Nondescript Other Such

Joe Szalinski

BookLeaf Publishing

india | USA | UK

Nondescript Other Such

Presentation by *BookLeaf Publishing*
Web: www.bookleafpub.com
E-mail: info@bookleafpub.com

ISBN: 9789358739169

First edition 2021

ACKNOWLEDGEMENT

I'd like to thank the publishers who rejected my pieces or didn't respond in a timely enough manner, which allowed me material for this book. I'd also like to acknowledge the significant and insignificant throughout life—all that influenced the writing herein. Also, a shoutout to the friends and family who like to make me feel like I maybe am a writer.

1. 'Murican Sen10ces

Karlheinz Stockhausen came from Sirius to deliver a message.

Romance isn't dead, it has just been reincarnated as wonder.

My humor is darker than the depths of space; starlight remains absent.

I cannot believe how lucky I am to have her wake up next to me.

This summer, one man will write a sentence with seventeen syllables.

Trees are the children, and I've adopted them to make art manifest.

"Anarchy, it's Greek to me," Plato commented, before going broke.

I am Joesus, the True, False Prophet; I demand no sacrifices, please.

Jerusalem Cruisers is a better name than just simply, sandals.

Who woulda guessed that happiness could be put on two wheels & ridden?

2. The Accident (Pantoum)

Small stones popped beneath the wheels

As we made our way around the gravel lot

The wagon was dragged behind us

Dust billowed in the air

As we made our way around the gravel lot

I heard the scraping of wood on stones

Dust billowed in the air

The load I hauled seemed lighter

I heard the scraping of wood on stones

Followed by the cry of children

The load I hauled seemed lighter

Kids lay scattered along the ground

Followed by the cry of children

I ambled about, disoriented

Kids lay scattered along the ground

Sarah, racked by sobs, was bleeding

I ambled about, disoriented

I found my way back to the wheel

Sarah, racked by sobs, was bleeding

Joey sprinted, carrying her in his arms

I found my way back to the wheel

And carted the children back to the house

Joey sprinted, carrying her in his arms

And was met by shocked parents

3. God

Couch sat in a thicket. Like it always had. Serving as an occasional resting place for hikers, insects, and all manner of life that needed to stop and rest on its sunken, dirtied cushions. Deer approached.

"Who are you?" asked Couch.

"God," replied Deer, "we all are."

"ME!?"

"If that's how you want to think of yourself. Yes. We are the same."

"God is everything? Even this question?"

Deer nodded, then stopped, noticing movement uphill. A prayer group, headed towards the woods for service, had startled wildlife, making them scatter; abandoning Couch like its owners who dumped it in mud.

4. Headphones Don't Ensure Privacy

With closed eyes

I donned headphones to

enjoy a little music

on the drive to Michigan.

The Beach Boys

were my usual go-to;

I memorized their lyrics

like important phone numbers

or my home address.

Singing along helped transport

me to Hawaii or Kokomo with them.

It also brought jeers

from my parents,

who were forced to listen,

held captive by locked doors

and seemingly endless stretches

of highway.

They'd come to mock me,

and my obliviousness—

of not knowing they could

hear every word.

Oh well...

they got a free concert.

5. Life (Ironic)

People lose theirs everyday,

yet we take it for granted.

Hell, there are already

too many humans on this planet.

We can select one of many facets

and become so involved.

It will appear to some

as if there's no life at all.

Death must be approaching

in order for us to be appreciative—

to take risks and take chances,

and allow our efforts to show initiative.

The more we experience it,

even shorter ours becomes.

Because living is really just dying,

isn't it, everyone?

6. Busia

You were an exceptional person,

who fought their battles fiercely.

And I would give all I could

just to have you near me.

For I remember the exact moment

I learned of your death.

Every atom of my being

became depressed & upset.

Confused as to what to do,

I looked for your help.

But the worst realization was,

I'd have to seek it from someone else…

And all these years later,

the pain hasn't subsided.

I've just learned how to move on,

find the feelings, and hide 'em.

Dwelling on losing you

prompted my first thought of suicide.

Though, I deemed the act fruitless,

being unsure of an afterlife.

But I don't need anything else

to feel your eternal love.

Because you supplied me your genes,

and I pump your Polish blood.

7. Poem

Here's a poem about

how this page is not a poem;

it's an advertisement for the book being read,

an intermission

Choose your own adventure

1) turn the page

2) close the book

8. A Hard Question for Soft Serve

My friends and I were baked to the gills, enjoying a few cones from Bruster's, when we heard a knock on the Pilot's window. I rolled it down to find three girls standing on the other side.

"Can we have your number?!" the leader of the pack asked.

I froze up. This situation was too good to be true. I stared blankly at them, under the assumption that this question was posed to my passengers as well. We sat there in silence.

"Guess not," said one of the other girls as they began to back away.

"Wait! Y-y-yes you can!" I replied desperately.

They came back to the window and asked if we had pen and paper. After searching briefly, I pulled out some, wrote my number down, and handed it to them.

As the girls pulled away, my buddies chirped from the back, "Don't they have cell phones? Why'd they need it written?"

9. Doggone Florida

My parents and I dissented from tradition,

and went to celebrate Xmas in Florida

with my sister and niece.

We travelled thru a slew of states,

stopping in Orangeburg, SC

to rest at a motel,

and to take a bathroom break in Georgia.

Our only detour in Florida,

was swinging by my pap's

in Homosassa,

having not seen him in a good while.

He filled us in on

recent goings on,

& recommended places to visit.

One that stuck out the most

was a restaurant with

an island full of monkeys!

I played with their new dog, Max

while the adults drank

& discussed stuff

beyond my years.

There were still bags to grab,

so my dad and I went to get them,

Max followed close behind,

seizing the opportunity

to flee thru an open door.

Pap paid little mind,

saying, "He does this all the time."

Time dragged on—no return…

not wanting us to come back

home to the sights & smells of

Max vomiting trash on the

front steps, Pap

drove off in his truck after him

Another period of eerie unease passed

before the screech of tires

tore thru the awkward tranquility.

Like a country song turned nightmare,

Pap erupted into the kitchen

swadling Max, who was tattooed

with tire tracks.

Incoherent sobs & expletives

showered the bloodied steps

and front door.

"I hit him! My poor buddy!

We need to get to a fuckin' vet!"

Calls were made;

the only available vet

was an hour away.

Pap was too distraught to drive,

my dad, a little tipsy,

but he persevered &

managed to pilot the truck

despite barely reaching the pedals.

Mel, my mom, and I

anxiously watched documentaries

in the interim.

10. Tools for Enlightenement

It Took Me Some Time To Realize That

The Art/Media I Exposed Myself To Wasn't The Sole *(blank), Or An Effective Prescription For Enlightenment. There're Permutations; Combos Of Art{i\e}facts Able To Produce Varying Results & Lead To New Insights, Depending On How/When Experienced—Since Doing So Simultaneously's Out Of The Question. Absorbing Multiple Pieces Of Media At Once, Waiting For Life To Intervene; Flourish The Framework, Like It Does Best.

*SOLUTION

11. Artsy Martyrs

The artsy martyrs take their positions

as cigarettes dangle from their mouths.

And smoke billows out like

the philosophies they erroneously espouse.

Expounding upon ideas,

can they follow a theme?

Society is far more cancerous

than their beloved nicotine.

12. Magician

Given a magic set as an early

b-day present one year,

I tore off

the cheap packaging

to find

mass-produced cards,

wand, hat, & gloves—

Smokey helped out

as my rabbit assistant.

After many

unsuccessful attempts at

conjuring things,

or making people disappear,

a career seemed fruitless!

How could I saw someone

in half if I struggled

with the basics?

All of this failure

left a bad taste in my mouth;

skepticism was a far heartier

& more delicious meal.

Now I stick on making magic

out of ink and paper.

13. Intelligence Test

"Everybody is a genius. But if you judge a fish by its ability to climb a tree, it will live its whole life believing that it is stupid."

-Probably Einstein

On a walk thru the woods to

our swimming spot,

the usual birdsong that

soundtracked our travels

was joined by sloppy flopping

at the roots of

swaying timber.

Exasperated fins and tails;

gills distressed due to

unkind environments;

struggled for escape from

evaporating puddles.

Refugees displaced by

strong storms—

fierce winds that

uprooted creature & water,

allowing the scaled exiles

to survive the violent transit

into the unfamiliar.

Rotting corpses eventually

drove my dad & I away, with their

putrid stench,

while attracting alien beasts

who'd liberate them from

misery in an act of ravenous mercy.

14. Odd Books

Here's to the odd books.

The ones that never fit into

any working scheme of what

reading was supposed to accomplish.

The random finds in secondhand

stores, or online, appearing

innocuous at first glance.

But really keep some sort of

secret hidden.

An ability to provide some

understanding of oneself

& the world.

15. 'Dos by Doobie

"Do you watch Batman, sweetie?" my mom asked as she examined the shaggy head of hair that sat in her barber chair.

"Yes," came a mousey reply from the little boy whose body shook after feeling the cold steel of the electric razor run against his neck.

"Well…" my mom continued, the hum of the razor silenced by the flip of a switch, "I need you to remain super still for this next part for me. Pretend Mr. Freeze froze you. Think you can do that?"

"Mhmm," squeaked the young boy, vigorously nodding in tandem, causing severed strands of hair to cascade to the floor below amidst a series of giggles.

I saw my mom employ this technique time and time again. Hell, I had even been duped into behaving just like everyone else. When presented as an exercise in imagination, a haircut didn't seem too scary or mundane.

16. I'm an awful Pittsburgher

I do not say "yinz" or "warsh" (Pittsburghese = not my thing

(although I do occasionally drop the "s" from East & West)

Fuck Iron City most of the time

Couldn't care less about sports
+but I will sport paraphernalia when required

Cannot find my way around this godforsaken city *

The Clarks can suck 12 sweaty donkey cocks...at once

-I'm sure they're nice people

*I can get lost anywhere, admittedly

17. A Helmet Can't Save You From Decapitation

The Rowdie Rooters,

local staple of Ross Township and North Hills School District.

A group of spirited partiers with a penchant for the boisterous and hilarious.

Attended by a cast of weirdos, sports fans, and miscreants of all stripes, meant that something interesting was always

bound to happen.

The guy in charge of t-shirts, a hippie,

usually invited the leftover Rooters to his place for

drinks and conversation.

Only, one Friday was a little different than the

others.

He had a party.

One guest, a terrified woman, who kept to herself

in the corner,

left that night in a rush—ready to lie to the police.

Early in the morning,

cops burst into his home and found him asleep.

They said they were told someone was murdered.

That he was seen arguing with someone and had

apparently cut off her head, and buried it in the

backyard.

The kicker, his hands were red from dyeing football shirts,

and there was a trail of it down the street and into the yard.

Police investigated and found a patch of ground covered by cement.

He was adding a driveway...

18. Take Me Home…Lang Road

Brendan's parents seemed kinda pissed that they had to pick the three of us up on a dirt-road at 2 am, but so would anyone! Especially all the way out in the backwoods of Sewickley!

We had no idea what we were doing out there. I did cruise around that area every so often. Usually not in weather so shitty, but it was a good place to turf yards and angrily stare at immaculate houses. It was my go-to place when I was bullied by boredom.

While at Eat N' Park earlier that night, we'd discussed our plan to drive to Florida over winter break for a bowl game, however, plans quickly changed…

Treacherous, icy hills were but mere obstacles for us and Brendan's four-wheel drive. He'd been boasting about drifting and exploiting the road conditions, so a hill was nothing. We were, admittedly, a little too cocky for such an undertaking. If only we'd listened to Han Solo's advice.

A little John Denver brings a good bit of bad luck to the listener. Substitute a tree for the Rocky Mountains, and an SUV for a plane, and we had our own crash—uphill, at a measly 5 miles per hour!

I'll never be able to forget Brendan screaming and pounding on the frozen ground; his buckled car sitting in a ditch, front-end making out with the bark of a gnarled, old tree; Shane suggesting we knock on the door to some random person's house; or me lying to the cop about having worn seat belts, as we waited for the tow truck.

19. Poetry Sucks

I can't stand poets,

or meters rhymed or not so.

Not big on most other artists either,

except the ones I've come to know.

There's entirely too much pretention

coming from such an uninspiring lot.

'Cause every really important poem,

masquerades as such, since it's not.

Poets who can't rhyme, write free-verse,

as do novelists who struggle with plot.

"Rhyming is for children, unless in a song,"

is some bullshit that we're taught.

Things can be funny and be heartfelt,

but can't remark on deep thought?

I'm picking fights with pedantic bookworms,

I'll keep it short, they're easily fought.

20. Book

Fuck yeah! You finished a book! I mean, it was only like 30-ish pages

       had weird formatting and w h i t e space,

but you finally did a thing!

Go reward yourself with something fun, like reading more of my stuff.

Or, get fucked up (if you're able to). Or don't. Pull a me and take a nap.

Burn this book even. Hell, I hope you stole it and used the open tome to shield your face from security cameras.

       This piece also only makes sense in the context of this book. Just imagine randomly seeing this in some shitty college poetry class or on some weird online forum, where it's fawned over by dastardly people with ghastly agendas.

Go write the next great poem or never pick up a
book again…but please, be haunted by this piece,
allow it to creep into your thoughts every so often
and keep you company in this mad world.